# SPEECHLESS

# SPEECHLESS

## REFLECTIONS FROM
## MY VOICELESS WORLD

### FIACRE RYAN

#### WITH ILLUSTRATIONS BY ALISON RYAN

MERRION
PRESS

First published in 2022 by
Merrion Press
10 George's Street
Newbridge
Co. Kildare
Ireland
www.merrionpress.ie

9781785374395 (Hardback)
9781785374425 (Ebook)

A CIP catalogue record for this book is available from the British Library.

Typeset in Sabon Lt Std 11.5/20

Cover design by Fiachra McCarthy

Upstart is an initiative of Mayo County Council Arts Service, and *Speechless* acknowledges the support received under this scheme.

Merrion Press is a member of Publishing Ireland.

To stay silent causes humans to be ignored and forgotten. I am speaking for all who are hidden in a world of outside shadows, waiting to restore their hearts and souls, waiting to be heard, waiting to be accepted.

# Carry On Dreaming

I am hugely daunted by this undertaking and I am scared to begin the writing of my book. Understanding autism asks a lot, but autism busies my mind all the time, so I have precious and unusual perspectives on life. I glean knowledge by observing my world: looking, imagining, seeing pictures and understanding life, breathing my air.

Having autism clears a world. Calm helps me to edit, and lasting words soothe my soul with dreams of writing my story. My raw awareness of my meaning and reasonings will resonate with all who struggle to be heard and valued as equals. Cutting-edge, inspiring writing of a real life living with autism.

Thank you to the people who supported me to find my voice. I am very happy dealing with imaginative, respectful people who sought to find a way to tell the story of my life. Know that

there are very many unusual life meanings still
to seek, and I will continue my search ...

# Introduction

My name is Fiacre Ryan.

I use a letterboard to communicate. Letter by letter sums up my mind's calm response to meaning. My life lets me hover between thoughts, yet I cannot speak. Telling my story is my gift to the world.

Believe that I attend to everything. When I was younger only some people could verify me. A mean response struck against intellect can make one very lonely. We insult each day, telling autistics to repeat tasks already repeated. The die is cast. It is a standard response: 'Not responded.' Repeat over. Better. Until brain ruptures ...

Sometimes good days come, and they are a taste of success. Having these successes gives me more incentive to be a testimony to autistic understanding.

In writing and poetry, I harness my thoughts and ideas. For me, inclusion is like an elusive party, you can't get in without an invitation. Not everyone sees the way I see the world, so not everyone gets invited.

Calm always brings my editing brain to life, bares my soul. I am being stopped in my thoughts when years of silence drown in turmoil and hold to ransom my autistic cure. Understand that daring to calm wet tears is futile, for cures are only attended in understanding.

Calm eases my deep voice and lets me mark those weary autism beliefs as evidence of being doubted. Don't articulate, warned to stay secret, while others decide my best interests. Yet I am capable of deciding for myself.

My world is totally transformed since I learned to communicate. It was cloudy and terrible and dark inside my thoughts. It was difficult to attend to rest when autism-attempted thoughts were revolting in my brain, gathering every day.

But a meeting of words, notes, spelling and typing has enabled my intelligence. RPM (Rapid Prompting Method) eases my anxiety, now I am resting in my long persistent respite, no longer daunted by attempts to have meaningful communication with the world.

Here now I tell my story, showing my understanding, reaching out, being respected, so people can listen to my world of turmoil. My thoughts unfurled on each page of my life story.

See the world through my eyes as I navigate through yours.

# Autism and Me

I'm afraid of people who feel that people with autism are less than others. The worst thing is that people think we are stupid. But we are people who understand so much. Let our opinions be heard.

The message some people try to write tells you many truths. Try to see past the autism and realise that we are the same inside as others.

I really only mostly try to show that I am not stupid.

I let the thoughts in my head seep to the letterboard and offer people reasons, beliefs and opinions, so that each one can understand my world.

# Branches and Bonfire

The seething branches cling to life as the
    volcanic aeons take hold,
tasting the sap seeping by as tall trees embering
    to their death,
searching the fire foes earthen ashes,
teasing to race wet wood.
Sparks attempt to sing soaring songs in the pit,
telling of stories that are their eaten branches as
    they taste a world of fettered yearning.
Yet they will die soon on the bonfire of
    remembrance,
ashed and wilted.

# What Family Means to Me

I live in a townland called Snugboro, a few kilometres from Castlebar, Co. Mayo. I am blessed with my family. My mum is Carmel, and my dad is Pat. My sisters are Rebekah (two years older than me), and Alison (nearly two years younger). In our family, dear names are attached to everyone, as a way of calling you affectionately. Thus, Carmel and the girls call me Fici, while Dad calls me 'chap' or 'boyzie'. It's a family thing really!

My family respects everything I want to achieve. My parents believe in me; they try to support me daily, even when others tell them to try other ways instead.

But our way is a super way, and it works amazingly for us. Mam has always worked really hard with me. It must exhaust her sometimes, but she never gives up. She tells everyone that I have a serious intellect, and encourages me to write. She restores me from my weary challenges and calms my stress. In the past people told her there was no point trying, but she did everything to help me learn and to help me communicate. When my breakthroughs came, she was proud and happy to see me at ease in my world.

Dad is my caring supporter. He always calms me when I am stressed. I believe that he will always be on my side when things are difficult in my life. We work very well together in the garden: strimming weeds, chopping and carrying in wood for the winter. In the evening we feed the horses and do all the outside farm work. As the evening light fades, I am relieved from all the stresses of the day, tired and fulfilled.

Some days are hard but Dad stays calm and supports me. At meetings he argues my autistic case with people who do not understand. Some people only believe their own prejudices, excluding me with no thought of a way back or a compromise to work towards. Even prisoners are considered for parole. Autism is a life sentence for those who committed no crime.

Surely everyone deserves a chance? One person can become the prosecutor, the judge and the jury. They hide their discrimination behind the protection of their positions, and others are afraid to call them out. Each person deserves to be treated with respect, and sometimes people need to be reminded about our autism and what it means. Dad always made sure of that, and for that I am forever grateful. Even on the darkest days, he was my rock, and always will be.

# Getting Stuck

New ideas try each day to wear me out.

Sometimes they never retreat,

sending me tested and stressed,

nowhere to escape them.

I become anxious, never stopping.

Usually I am searching, more tense;

I cannot control my ideas, a hamster on a wheel

    of thoughts.

Stress lives through weary reasons I can't

    explain.

Stuck on my noted mind's tatters, as I try in

    vain to move on.

# Education

It only seems appropriate to give the same rights given to those without autism, to individuals with it. Needing some type of assistance does not make someone less of a person. Being different does not impact my label of human. I am the living product of the most human quality in all. Begin to teach and learning can occur.

Autistics like me usually do not stay in school. Yet my parents would strive to wear out all opposition; to allow me to be understood, respected. And given the chance to be a student like each other boy.

The Leaving Cert is a serious attempt to become an autistic understood; worth causing a war with believers who belittle our cause.

We deserve a breakthrough, studying useful subjects and taking exams, showing everyone we deserve the same opportunities as our peers.

A life ambition can be achieved. Dare to

dream. It's important for me to do my Leaving Cert. I am like all my peers, needing to prove my intelligence to the world.

# First Day at Secondary School

Busy days filled with books,

Going from class to class with some looks,

Always on the move,

Getting myself to prove,

Having so much to learn,

Liking it because now it's my turn.

# Body and Mind

Each one has a story to tell, and needs someone to tell it. The story of my life is a search for understanding and acceptance. Believe in minds that work differently, like my mind. We are better talkers and thinkers than people realise. We pay attention in our measured world. We have a knowledge most people find amazing.

We are challenged to fit into a world that has no rest from weary turmoil. See the world through our eyes, as we navigate the world through yours.

Be kind and respect our difference, and restore our place in society as useful human beings, with our uniqueness. Believe in me to carry out my goals through many disabilities into the future. My body has challenges but my mind is intact.

# School Challenges

Yes, I cry each day – autism wet tears. Stupid useless autistic waste. Yet I am awesome.

I am so weary and bored doing stupid autism things at the unit. Others eat their lunch each day at the canteen but I am always at the unit, alone.

Each day others see me outside calming myself, trying to pass the test. Tell them I am very stressed, yet I am always on my own. The stress beats down on my calm body, sending it into turmoil and hopelessness.

Days could stop at school. A rapid test could cut my days short, the tape on the camera is running a trial of my serious incidents with evidence to send me home.

# SPEECHLESS

# Understand the Different

Teenager sees how I am,

Sees yet each teenage want,

Taught to spell some reasons with his sayings,

With his telling of each story to use codes

And to reach the world.

He reasons and tells sad tales of history,

When people were persecuted and
    exterminated,

And he reckons that some still try to silence the
    ones who are different.

Talk is our utmost difference,

And we are silenced when we spell what others
    do not want to know.

# Striving

This is my time to work, to be a totally normal student, to taste what others experience the whole time. So I tend to the study of history, taking in all the knowledge.

Understand that the one who cannot speak tries to type but every day is a struggle to be fast enough to do my exam. That estranges me from every other boy in my class who can tell the answers that I try to tell. Some people don't know their easy life; they complain about trivial stuff. I wouldn't be so ungrateful.

You were born to strive, to achieve your best. I'm trying to do that with the support of my family and my teachers and all the people who believe in me.

# A Note to My Mother

Once upon a time, there was an intelligent boy
    who only tried to talk.
No words joined him, so he only stopped
    trying.
He looks normal mostly, but he gazes at things.
No one enters his thoughts, only him.
He is lost in his mind, like me.

# Thoughts on Tests

Yet again I attend to testing, catering to the universal thinking about autism. Each test is knowledge that I am limited with a data search, wasted and useless, not heard and understood.

Tests are neurotypical, and I am not typical. I am unable to speak, voiceless. See me, each test takes away belief.

Caution, and re-test in a different way, then see my autistic brain show my intelligence.

# SPEECHLESS

# Revision and Preparation

Attending to my exam prep caused me stress. Each day Mam and Claire, my RPM tutor, revised subjects with me through past papers. Doing the answers prepared me but I could only pray that decent questions would come up.

Macbeth's evil and malevolent atmosphere and characters (I especially liked the witches), the angst-filled poems of Emily Bishop, a poignant 'Begin' by Brendan Kennelly, Yeats's death obsession causing him to miss the living – all these thoughts colliding around each mind's turmoil, day after day.

Maths is always easy for me: watching algebra, forming answers, understanding all, using my cortex brain to tame a hypothesis on the page.

History, a part of our world, having a lesson for us all from a time of old, we remember and attend to. Geography is my least favourite, and I have a lot left to work on for a grade.

My weeks are weary, calming being beyond my brain and my body, but verifying my intellect is my goal.

# To the Library

Walking to the library,
Past buildings old and new,
Wind whistles by the curling edge of leaf,
Through trees shadowed blue.

Lights are flickering,
Photocopier humming,
I hear the sound
Of a child's fingers drumming.

The spine of my book,
I hold it terrified,
My thoughts and words in print.
Now I am verified.

# Exam Results

A life ambition can be achieved. Dare to dream.

Each day I went to the centre, calming myself so that every time I answered the papers I would be able to show all that I had studied. All my family and friends were supporting me.

Even though I went on the bus most days, Mam always supported me from her place in the bushes, since, I think, she was accused of being critical of a principal and could not go to the centre. Calming prayers reached my soul.

Racing thoughts ran their course, once I started. Every belief strengthened me, made the test hard, but support carried me beyond the obstacles, beyond those who tried to prevent me.

Believe that very stupid men have turtle shells that they hide within, emerging to instigate lies and aspersions. However, they tried in vain. Cowards and cynics will not now cast aspersions on me, the results are there to see:

| Subject | Level | Grade |
|---|---|---|
| English | Ordinary Level | 3 |
| Mathematics | Ordinary Level | 1 |
| History | Ordinary Level | 3 |
| Geography | Ordinary Level | 4 |

By creating these tests autistic students are excluded from some subjects. A change in attitude from those who should try to support me is warranted. They see only what they want to see.

I see a world where my testimony can help to cure their narrow minds.

# Spring Walk

Cold drops of snowflowers emerge ground torn
    huddled,
cast out beneath tree carpets.
Bark fungus looks like Autumn beastly curled,
Calling insects to roam in its foam.
Sticky catkin buds tell of life
Secretly hiding every day,
Waiting to reveal, hastening to leaf.
Crocus bursts orange crush petals by a stump.
Early daffodil ragged wind – torn, broken –
Tries to hold up her head.
Teased by each gust she stays,
A promise of strength.
Spring will come always, after Winter despair.
Believe a swan's love story at Turlough waters.
Hope returns.

# Why was it important to do the Leaving Cert?

It was important for me to do my Leaving Cert; a serious attempt to become an autistic understood. The thought of having an education and then nothing at the end caused me such stress. I am like all my peers, needing to prove my intelligence to the world.

Discussions about doing my exams kept distracting me as I was preparing, sometimes causing me to regret my decision, and led me to question the minds of people supposed to be supporting me. Being negative, setting obstacles which I would have to remove. Hearing that I couldn't verify my knowledge seriously restored and always attended to my determination to succeed. Hating only conversations about my autism, cancelling my intellect in one phone call or email. Always my brain can recall each fact, and retain my learning.

Autistics like me usually do not stay in school. Yet my parents strove to wear out all opposition to allow me to be understood, respected, and given the chance to be a student like each other boy cutting past each obstacle in the path.

The hardest thing was being different all the time in school. The exams were wearying but being different means people will add to your weariness. Do not cry worthless tears – each one weeps – yet autistics weeping are cast aside when they might fail in school and show their difference to the system. We are hidden within worlds of silence, walls of the system.

Autism attends to stress like trees standing on their roots, tall and strong, yet showing weak, wet stress when a storm wreaks havoc, destroying branches and limbs. Where vain attempts to be calm weary their souls, testing their very existence.

Do you want to know the worst thing? Not having the opportunity to partake in my own life decisions, not being called like others to realise my hopes and dreams, casting me aside each time someone says I am too slow at getting my thoughts to paper.

My brain decided to show that marvellous and beautiful thoughts deserve to be respected. My determination held fast, my stress calmed and my body restored itself daily.

The Leaving Cert seeks to grade intelligence.

I am now graded as normal.

# The Story of My Life

The reason I live tells a story of believing that each one belongs to the world, yet some are not heard.

Thoughts are yearning to escape with each story I attempt to weave, with thoughts crashing between day and night, saying silent words over and over, believing each attempt will keep my turbulent thoughts at peace.

Yearning for belonging, celebrating utmost data in autism turrets in my head, and attesting to calming waters calling to me in my dreams.

There I am my true self, daring to be alive and understood.

# SPEECHLESS

# Swan Eulogy

Calming peace, day ended
swans tiny feet deep beneath
water wetlands, rose,
caused startling cacophony,
calling to cue.
To attend may call to one a
death,
swansong,
resting,
never again to see a wave lap on
eyrie bed,
swan swims alone for eternity.
My writing too like a cymbal crash
in my life, a sudden sound rising, each
attempt at understanding, a ransom's search
    each silent day.
I paddle under waves
treading deep bobbing anxiety,
wet tears, yet each day, surviving.

# Being Silent

When I was sixteen, I wrote an article called 'Finding my voice':

> I am a student with autism who uses a communication board, communicating my thoughts by seeping words from my brain to others. I want to explain the mind of someone who cannot speak; a testimony to a student who understands, and showing the zenith of my intelligence. Speech is the most wanted thing, yet no words form for me. Sounds try to escape; zealous thoughts try to break through the silent whispering of my world. Some thoughts rest there, and some thoughts escape in spellings on my letterboard. Each time I tell a piece of my story only heard through silent spoken words, written as I edit each sentence, I share understanding with others. Each time

the door opens on a new day I am doubted, but each day I prove my strong mind to everyone and yet they try to stop me from using this intellect. Respect those who speak silent words, who have thoughts lost in their minds, and show them what every person sees as we tell our story. When I first started spelling, I wrote to my mother 'There was once a boy who tried to speak. No words joined him, so he only stopped trying.' Now I like to think that I am verifying people with autism when I write my thoughts. The world tells me to live the way others live but I am not in their world. I exist every day through the world of autism, which causes me to understand everything completely different to their world. Yet I am the student who understands the world better than the rest.

Now, years later, I look back at how my life has emerged from silence. My world has completely transformed since I learned to communicate. It was cloudy, terrible and dark inside my thoughts. It was very difficult to rest when thoughts were revolting in my brain, gathering every day. But with a meeting of words, my spelling and typing has enabled my intelligence. Seeping screams communicate each thought, letting turmoiled sentences grow. I am no longer daunted by attempts to have meaningful conversation with the world. Daring to place my thoughts on a page is a long, difficult process. Some might say mastering the letterboard freed my thoughts,

but I believe it tamed them. Before I learned to communicate they were determined to wreak havoc, catapulting like a tsunami around my brain. Challenging me to control them.

Now I can marshal this kaleidoscope into formation, tumbling letters into words, and transfixing them on a screen. Meaning comes to life in typed text. I marvel yet again as a voice speaks each sentence that I craft.

Day breaks, awakening, and calm descends, bringing with it my utmost rest.

# One Summer's Evening

The sea seeps along the sandy shore,

Washing stones,

Attracting sunlights' rays,

Turmoil in the waves,

Tossing seaweed to the earth.

Taking memories of our family holiday to a
horizon.

Yet we will remember the sandcastle built
regally,

Testimony to cousins digging together in the
sands.

A white feather and a red rose,

Seared in yesterday's weary efforts to hold back
the waves.

Yesterday's castle,

Today's calm sea tide.

# What Nature Means to Me

I am at peace with nature. Tears never darken my door when I am outside. Destined to never speak, I am calm when nature envelops me in her soothing world, and gives my senses peace. These things are special to me.

To walk on the beach, for there I see waves teeming towards distant shores, flicking my toes, sand underfoot, telling of each who has walked here before. In the water, staring, ripples wash over my feet, soothing the testing waves to the rocky shore. Sand stretches golden for miles before me. As I walk into the salty wind, away from all worries, seagulls soar above me, we are free.

Returning home I seek to cut twigs with my hands and ooze out the sap in my sticky fingers, wet and real. Thistles sting my hand as I touch twigs, carving them into strips of fresh bark. Grass flicking; my escape from stress. Every note of birdsong soothing my spirit. Bees buzzing their tales of summer, scent of roses in bloom. I am dancing every day to my own magical meaning.

# Nature and Me

Believe that nature restores my weary soul.
Being rooted at a scene of natural beauty,
    heron – resting and listening to a woody
    symphony,
Basking in sunray's warm glow as the rest of
    life is silenced.
Beach tide crashes my thoughts causing me to
    up the beat of my dance between the waves,
    sand – flicking my toes.
By evening's fading light we cut wood and
    stoke a fire, homaging the starry skies.
All the elements call to me.
Content.

# SPEECHLESS

# My Love of Nature

Dare to be peaceful each day.

Dare to be well.

Dare to live satisfied.

Nature stills my anxious soul.

Hating to be made to stay inside,

Being tested,

Called to count cubes.

Cloudy windows hide pouring rain,

As my mind wanders out to wet twigs and
    sodden leaves,

Nature's rest nears.

Later I walk,

Rain tapping Glorias on window panes,

Stress vanishes with each step,

My myriad coloured world.

# Treasure Hunt

The world outside sears with possibilities, where a person can search for each calm to get washed treasures, teeming with raindrops, padded fears, under a blue world. Testimony to my aesthetic world, vast and beautiful.

# My Horse Charlie

My world becomes better when I ride, carefree, seeing a scene outside that passes by, moment by moment. A horse sees everyone the same.

Charlie walks the fields silently, noble and faithful, munching sweet green grass. Head turning as we arrive, he gallops to greet us, hooves thudding, mane flying: powerhorse. Neighing, standing tall, he waits until I mount, and together we ride the wind. Master and companion, in motion, partners and friends.

Understand that talk easily misses what daring thoughts are in my heart, when animals understand my brain, that it can weep, and tears seep every day. That's why I am easily angry. Only with talking here can I save what I cannot have: my mind at rest.

# My Garden

Each person attends his garden to restore
    nature's story to earth.
Each person belongs in a garden, taking time
    to feel the earth beneath his fingers, feeling
    alive.
Carting stones to warm, covered, cushion-
    raised beds,
Gravel grating shovelling,
My arms tired, voting to stop,
Break time.
Compost enriched soil,
Fertilised now with Charlie's hay – eaten
    manure.
Each cycle of nature wheels the season in my
    garden.
I am lime chalk path carrying soil to nurture
    seeds,
Each bed cotton soft dream to stalk and leaf,
Restored to beauty.

# SPEECHLESS

Dad's hands in mine – potato planting, strong,
Working together,
Our time.

# Storm Ophelia

.

Tumultuous cauldrons ascend tearing the
    sycamore
Wet branches
Deep swells
Caves erupt
Dare this theatre
Enter Ophelia
Storms siren
Hamlet's girl
Swathes of wet clouds reel back
Peeling wreckage
Ophelia
Tempest under the hell on earth.

# My Family

My great mother has helped me with everything. Getting really hard news when your son is small has to have called for some courage. Having courage in the face of difficulties is really something that gives me solace in getting through hard moments. I learned how to do this from my mother. I hardly ever stress about stuff now because my mother always has my plan worked out. Her attitude has helped me to do really hard things like learning how to express myself.

Over the years Mam made life happy for myself, Alison and Rebekah. I really have been lucky with Dad too. He never ever does anything to make me feel that I need to have a different personality or be like everyone else. I need to say that the way my Dad looks at me is really so powerful and gives me unusual confidence. Being myself is the only way I can have joy.

Doing a lot of things with my sisters is what

will stay in my memories. Although they can be a challenge at times when they get bossy.

I'm not sure at all how I would manage without sisters like them. I really love everyone in my wonderful family. I have incredible confidence because of them.

# Looking Back and Moving Forward

Mam says I was diagnosed with autism when I was attending my local mainstream playschool. I was very lively and had very little sense of danger!

At the age of five I started in the Newport school ASD (Autism Spectrum Disorder) unit, the nearest one to me. They say it takes a village to raise a child, but I had two villages: Snugboro and my adopted Newport. The teachers there helped and included me in all of school life.

After a long bus ride, my days were filled with activities: swimming, baking, making things, art, computers, and lots of parties. There were many trips to the playground and around the town. Sunshine days in my memories, feeling loved, respected, included, belonging. I miss those carefree times.

Even though I could not speak, there was

always someone to attend to my needs. When I started on my letterboard, everyone was excited for me, and trained in using RPM, a new method, with open minds. I progressed quickly and was soon able to join project groups and show that I had been learning all along.

Education is about being taught, and I was steeped in knowledge. Teach us appropriately and everyone can learn.

\* \* \*

Secondary School was a melting pot of experiences. I settled in well with the help of my SNA (special needs assistant), Cathy, who was caring and kind, and brilliant at understanding and supporting me. I hovered between mainstream and the unit, on the margins of school life.

I wanted to gain respect, not pity; to be like everyone else, and to study the same subjects. However, there were times when some decisions and timetables tested my anxiety. Tension mounted when I wanted to do my exams, as this had not been done before. Narrow minds behind wide doors. There were meetings, phone calls and emails, but this was my decision. My parents made sure that I would have the same chances as every other student.

In 2019 I duly became the first non-verbal autistic student to sit my Leaving Cert exams. I am truly grateful to the people who believed in me. For many years people like me were denied an education. 'A mind is a terrible thing to waste,' and I intend to continue my studies further. Autism will not stop me from realising my dreams.

# Ben Bulben

I see Ben Bulben, a mountain bare and majestic.
Looking down at Drumcliff's graves, a tall cross
    of ancient times, a church nearby.
Pathways of old, witness to ancestors long
    gone.
No marble tombstone, yet stone cut words tell
    his story of life and death, his final resting
    place.
I see the calm evening sunlight of the Lissadell
    estate.

## SPEECHLESS

The windows of the Great House are open
     to the South, two beautiful sisters in silk
     kimonos taking in the view, one tall and
     one graceful like a gazelle.
The air is still and the evening shadows fall.
But calm is burdening,
and death tames all.

# Adult Education

When I left school, I applied to the NLN (National Learning Network) in Castlebar, a centre for adult learning. I had attended to my studies and achieved a test confirmation of my intellect. But having intelligence is only a part of weathering a life of useful existence.

Attending to my adult education centre occupies my days now. My programme is all about catering for myself for the future. Cooking for myself, buying my groceries, being understood and independent are all the skills I need help with to develop fully. Independence makes people respect me and so I need to learn more life skills. Sometimes good days come and they are a taste of success.

An education carries on through all our life.

Calling it by another title tests me each day to search to do more independent work. I am an adult learner all my life, finally holding the title raises expectations. I strive to learn skills that will assist me to achieve valuable opportunities in life. Having a support system makes my attempts and goals realistic. My adult brain does the thinking, and I try each day to train my autistic body to behave like someone who is called normal.

Attend to my autism support. I thank teachers who respect my difference and see my value in society.

# The Hermit Saint

The hermit skeleton sits alone in an ancient cave.

Dying as he lived, prayer about tonsured head,

eyes open, remembering thoughts and stories of
   a holy man

what secrets buried with him, comforter of
   wounded souls.

His fasting ended up with sweet berries and
   gifted a honey thanks,

barefoot mountain path home

hard leaf and sheep's wool flagstone bed,
   penance for others pleasures

telling the secrets of the past to the people we
   are today,

saving the story that we all share

Everyone passes through when they die,

taking their thoughts with them, waiting to
   wake from rest.

Longing for the peace of the dying hermit saint,

the holy man.

# SPEECHLESS

# My Experience of Living with Autism

People ask all the time what it is like living with autism. But I have never known any other life apart from this one.

I am redefining what autism means. Challenging the age-old perceptions. Analysing how my brain and body disconnect, since my brain attends to my body chaotically, my neural pathways skewed.

A thought escapes. All the particles collide like the Large Hadron Collider, accelerating through the tunnel of my brain, nearing light speed, hurtling along my body. Trying so hard to be useful, neurotypical, even normal. But the thoughts revel in chaos, sending the body into eccentricities, nothing like intended.

A collision with a great fallout; a scattering of particles. Eyes are now all on me, the day is ending badly. Just a typical autistic moment of interacting forces, out of my control. Tension takes over, stress envelops every core of my being, wearing me down, eventually hosting anxiety, dancing around my brain, echoing a roared chaos, a dreaded nightmare. Calm returns too late in the day to save me. Exclusion awaits, again.

It is too easy to exclude people who cannot speak up for themselves. We have a right to be treated with respect. Our opinions matter, our lives matter. No one has the right to silence our unheard voices. To shut us out of our own lives. Talked about, doubted, dismissed. Calling us names, deciding our fate, while we can only listen.

Believe that our brains colliding in catalysts will one day astound those decision makers who seek to deny us.

# Richard

There was a man called Richard who knew everything there was to know about autism. He would share his knowledge with everyone.

'Did you know autistic people can't understand language?' he said to the teachers at the conference. The next day, while on the phone to the mother of an autistic child, he said, 'You shouldn't put your effort into making your child the best he can be. There won't be much progress so don't waste your time.'

The next time he spoke to his colleagues he said, 'They don't understand what objects are, so how are they supposed to understand concepts?' He was the expert so no one dared to question him, until one day when he came across a non-verbal autistic person who pointed on a letterboard to share his inner thoughts.

'You know nothing,' he spelled. That was one expert told and many more to go.

# Covid-19

Covid-19 asks everyone to cancel normal life. Do not visit anyone. Only essential trips are permitted. I haven't seen my granny and I miss her daily presence in my life. Each day I worry that someone in my life will die from this evil deadly viral infection.

The air we breathe has become our enemy, spreading vicious secret coronavirus tear droplets, casting out the weakest in our world. Each one must do their part to stop the spread. Each one understands hand hygiene rules, social distancing. Wearing a mask is each one's responsibility to avoid passing a particle of the disease.

We are not allowed contact with our friends. I miss getting in the car to go to the shop. Now Mam makes me walk miles for ice-cream.

When this is all over, I will go to Spain – back to a normal life, only better!

# Coronavirus

Each new word,
Anxietitious virilus contagious,
Baring tears of the isolated
lost covid-darkest bleakest
ending life.
Quarantine rested death,
dare to call at my door,
I am a weary social isolator,
rabid and kept at a distance,
waiting and longing for inclusion.

Ironic isn't it corona,
See all behave like autistics now.

# SPEECHLESS

# What is My Life Like Now?

My life is slowly getting back to normal after the covid lockdowns. Being autistic, it was more difficult for me. Having weeks crawl painfully by eats away at my mind and my soul. Thoughts turmoil through my head, relentless.

Returning activities calm me, and my spirit is being restored. Attending my adult education centre occupies my days now. I am an adult learner all my life, finally holding the title raises expectations. I strive to learn skills that will assist me to achieve valuable opportunities in life.

Having a support system makes my attempts and goals realistic. My adult brain does the thinking, and I try each day to train my autistic body to behave like someone who is called normal.

# The Morning Light

The red flowers collect around my door
    changing each and every day,
more radiant than before.
I watch cautiously as the bees sit about.
I begin to hum their tune as the morning light
    awakens
and hides the last glares from the moon.
The day is fresh now,
people are moving,
the gift of day has begun.
Tension mounts as traffic snarls
    and snakes along the city streets.
Sirens call hospitals to ready.
Buses screech the latest news.
Everyone scurrying to work or school, clock-
    minding.
Breakfast wafts,
bagels baking,
coffee waking.

Cars scramble to park, scooters whizz by.

Mothers pushing sleepy baby buggies in the
    park,

like ducks swimming in lines and circles,

feet paddling beneath.

All life assembled.

I slip into the shadows, for my time on earth is
    done.

Until the light begins again.

# After the Documentary

Dreams belong to people who believe in miracles. Thank you for listening and attending to my dreams.

Since *Speechless* (the RTÉ programme), I have become an accidental advocate. People realise now that I have a voice, speaking for those with a hidden disability, and my voice is being heard. A parent wrote to me, 'Thank you for sharing your story, and for shining a light on a world with ASD' (Autism Spectrum Disorder). I was very touched and deeply humbled by the messages I received, from all over the country and abroad.

Many people took the time to write messages of support and congratulations to me. There was an outpouring of love for my wonderful caring family, making me proud that I am their son and brother. Trending on Twitter and all across social media, and reaching number one on the RTÉ Player was awesome!

However, this brings with it the responsibility to use my words wisely, and make a difference wherever I can. For far too long we have managed to survive with sparse services, seeking out our own support. Count us as useful members of society, educate us appropriately, and support us in employment, and in our communities.

The neurotypical voice seeks to edit my story, trying to set my words in their own mindset, daring to change my thoughts into their own beliefs and opinions. Understand deep chasms are between their testimony and mine, as I am the one who lives this life. It is harmful, violent even, to dismiss our rights; our rights to have a different opinion to yours. It is our life; please have the sensitivity to respect our uniqueness, and help all autistics to be accepted, valued and understood.

# Goals for the Future

I would like to tell the world my thoughts and words; weeping tears, yet casting each thought to people who will listen. I want to write my life story so that understanding will verify people like me who belong in the world of intellect. Day to day, we may appear really tense and cause trouble, yet useless we are not. We are autistic in our bodies, not in our brains.

My brain confirms me as a writer with awesome stories and poetry, saturating, teeming with ideas. See that my sayings are written and that education continues, so that I can do exams and go to college, and study history and politics. Believe in me to carry out my goals through many disabilities, into the future. My body has challenges, but my mind is intact.

I am persisting at typing skills so that I can type my thoughts by myself. I want to make my own decisions about my life. Nothing is impossible if I get support and understanding. Independence makes people respect me and so I need to learn more life skills. Working at proper paid employment could even make me rich!

Believe that I will attend to writing my story. My life has been stressful, calm has eluded me. Many events do not matter to me, yet I am called to them.

Life has many challenges and opportunities. I would like to study a college course in English and creative writing. Poetry is my passion. I think all forms of poetry are beautiful, and are a true expression of a real message from the poet to the people.

I would like to have my own house in the future, and have people recognise me as being human, calm and fulfilled.

Many people are interested only in always being looked at as cool. My mindset is different because no one thinks that I am cool, so I am not wasting time trying to impress people with that.

I'm using my energy to work on more

important things, like having realistic goals. Staying positive is the most important thing.

Negative thoughts cause me anxiety. Because doubts become like truths. And I am obsessed with these thoughts and I can't stop them.

I used to worry because people are not understanding; but a better way is to find a positive thought and to relax at a better place in my head and my responses. It feels paralysing sometimes, but each day I am trying new ways to stress less, and I feel calmer then.

I long for inclusion, where people listen to the voice of those who are no longer silent. I speak in my writing, testimony to my story in my autistic world.

# SPEECHLESS

# Family

Family all together at last.
Evening light descends on the dinner table,
    bathed in candle glow.
Voices raised in laughter and story, a cauldron
    of fun.
Honeymooners hand-fastened in love.
Delicious smells wafting from the kitchen, the
    promise of a feast.
Wine-clinking, a toast to our health and
    happiness.
Chatter calms to a steady hum of appreciation,
    dinner is served.
Sated after, I sit in a comfy couch.
I listen to tales of foreign lands, drinking from
    the enthusiasm of youth.
Here I am safe;
believed, accepted and understood.

# SPEECHLESS

# New Horizons

I have become an accidental advocate for autism awareness. There is still so much more to learn about autism, and especially the brain of one who does not speak.

Recently I was privileged to take part in a Cambridge University UK research project: 'Hidden Abilities in Autism', to measure my brain's response to language, using brain imaging technology, with Dr Alex Woolgar and Dr Selene Pettit. This research is particularly valuable as much of the previous research into autism is about autistics who are verbal. They do not study one who does not speak.

Our heroes raise us up on their shoulders, inspiring us to live our best lives, and I am fortunate to meet my hero, Temple Grandin. Dr Grandin is a prominent author and speaker on both autism and animal behaviour. She says 'the world needs all kinds of minds', and that includes my unique mind, and my garbled wired-up brain.

I have been invited to present at the Beyond Limits event in October, from the office of the Ombudsman for Children. That should be a challenge for technology!

I believe that there are no limits to what young people with a disability can achieve, we just need to believe in ourselves, and for others to believe in us.

# The Future

I did not choose this life, rather I believe it chose me. It blessed me with dreams and ambitions, and hope for the future. I have achieved many 'firsts' in my life, and I will continue trying to break down boundaries.

My dream of becoming a writer is unfolding, and I am sharing my unique perceptions of my world.

I would like to write speeches, with words that help people to understand autism better; to travel and see the world, savouring the sights and sounds of myriad cultures; to be accepted into university and study history and creative writing.

Later I would like to buy a house by the sea, where I would wake each morning to the sound of waves lapping my door, and the promise of beach walking days to come.

My dreams are many, but I believe they

may indeed come true. Living this life well, I can inspire others to achieve their dreams, a life without limits.

# Acknowledgements

Thank you to the wonderful team at Merrion Press and especially to Patrick O'Donoghue, whose vision was a driving force at all times with his unfailing belief in my voice as a writer and poet.

Thank you to the people who brought the documentary *Speechless* to life: Colm O'Callaghan of RTÉ, Christine Thornton and Mark Warren of Firebrand Productions, Bonnie Dempsey, Liam McGrath and Gretta Ohle.

My sincere gratitude to all the people throughout Ireland who sent letters, cards and messages of appreciation and encouragement.

To my fellow RPM friends, thank you for sharing this journey with me. To Soma Mukhopadyay, Erika Anderson, Sue Finnes, Alex Hopwood and Claire Philbin for sharing your expertise with me.

To the Fanning and Ryan families, thank you for your love and support. A very special thanks to my sisters, Rebekah and Alison, who help me every day; to Alison for the beautiful illustrations, and to both of you for putting up with me!

And finally the greatest thanks to Mam and Dad for always believing in me, for helping me to believe in myself, and for never giving up on me.

Fiacre Ryan